MARIN

FARM FAMILIES

Alex Hinds, *Director*
Marin County Community Development Agency

Barbara Marino, *Writer*

Ken Smith, *Photographer*

Susan Bercu, *Designer & Illustrator*

Elisabeth Ptak, *Editor*

Special Thanks to
Marin County Board of Supervisors
Susan Adams, *District 1*
Hal Brown, *District 2*
Charles McGlashan, *District 3*
Steve Kinsey, *District 4*
Cynthia Murray, *District 5*

STORIES & RECIPES

COUNTYWIDE PLAN 2006, SUPPORTING DOCUMENT

Cover insert photo: Stewart Campbell, great grandson of the late legendary cattleman Boyd Stewart, shows off one of his two Holstein heifers. He's raising them himself because he wanted to be assured of a way to get his own milk for making yogurt and ice cream since his family's ranch specializes in Angus beef cattle.

Cover background photo: Allstar Organics, Nicasio

Inside front cover photo: Farmland, Novato

Inside back cover photo: Box A Ranches, Tomales

Published by Marin County Community Development Agency
3501 Civic Center Drive, Room 308 San Rafael, California 94903

ISBN Number 1-4243-0319-2
Printed in China
Recycled paper ♻

Contents

I would like to thank the tireless, always extraordinary, farming and ranching families who allowed me into their homes, barns, trucks, and all manner of unique meeting places to discover how vital they are to the health, harmony, and heart of Marin County. I'd also like to thank Ann Corda who gave me good guidance, our hands-on, always-a-delight editor Elisabeth Ptak, whose love of good words is equal only to her love of these stories of farming families, Dick Jordan for reviewing the recipes, and the wonderfully talented team of Susan Bercu and Ken Smith whose design and photography turned words into art.

~ Barbara Marino

We are pleased to include in this collection recipes created by Amy Nathan Weber, Peggy Smith, Gerald Gass, and other food professionals who live or work in West Marin. But for the most part, the recipes you will find here have not been tested in any kitchens but the ones belonging to the families who have provided them. No one can vouch for the cakes and pies or the stews and roasts described in these pages except the generations who have enjoyed them at weekday lunches or Sunday dinners. The ingredients are sometimes straight from the field, like David Little's Pouch Potatoes, and sometimes straight from the pantry like the stale French bread used to make Mamma Grossi's Bread Soup. In every case, they are the product of a desire to satisfy a hunger for good food made with love for family and friends. Enjoy.

~ Elisabeth Ptak

Alex Hinds

Director, Marin County Community Development Agency

Ever since the Gold Rush brought a wave of new settlers to California in the mid-1800s, working farms and ranches have contributed greatly to Marin's beautiful and diverse landscapes. While much has changed over the years, the agricultural community continues to play a critical role in defining Marin's exceptional quality of life.

In its most recent update, the Marin Countywide Plan builds on a long legacy of creative collaboration between agricultural and environmental interests and carries this tradition one step further by celebrating the farm families themselves. Toward this end, we hope this "Addendum to the Marin Countywide Plan" will provide increased insight into the men and women who provide such generous opportunities for us to enjoy the fruits of their labor.

It is their way of life, not the sometimes small financial returns, that keeps most Marin farming and ranching families in the business of feeding others. Luckily for us, as a result of their commitment to a variety of sustainable agricultural stewardship practices, they also typically provide healthier, higher quality food products. Many of these family farmers employ a wide variety of environmentally sound practices including rotational grazing, fencing of creek conservation areas, organic certification, silage production, deferred grazing during times critical to plants and wildlife, grass-fed livestock husbandry, and dry farming. As a result, fewer natural resources

Alex Hinds

are consumed and environmental contamination is largely minimized or avoided. By helping maintain healthy agroecosystems, Marin's agricultural community is a fundamental building block for supporting sustainable communities and reducing our ecological footprint.

We hope you will enjoy the farm family stories and recipes included here, as well as the rich variety of vegetables, fruits, herbs, oils, meats, dairy products, oysters, and other delectable goodies grown or produced in the Marin County foodshed. In addition to the inherent value in better understanding the cultural component of agriculture—along with my irresistible urge to create a fun, coffee-table-style general plan document—our real agenda is to increase your appreciation of and financial support for local agriculture. Enabling our existing dairies, farms, and ranches to stay in business, also helps retain our quality of life and keeps our communities authentically connected to this 150-year-old heritage.

So please don't forget to slow down, eat locally, and enjoy the working landscapes of Marin County. We can all benefit from the experience.

Stacy Carlsen

Marin County Agricultural Commissioner

The term sustainability evokes numerous definitions that attempt to describe an exacting set of criteria and procedures for success. But the term is evasive, perhaps because the components of sustainability are unique to each grower, farm, and community. There is no one-size-fits-all. The challenge is to understand the values and objectives of the many individuals attempting to reform modern agricultural practices. Changing the current paradigm of high input, resource consumption, and environmental degradation will require developing shifts in attitudes, farming practices, and government policies.

To become entwined in our everyday life in Marin County, sustainable agriculture must be fostered by the farmers' commitment to the land, supported by local markets, and buoyed by public policy that encourages back-to-the-future philosophies and practices. Success relies on continuous and direct interaction between growers, land, community, local government, and the market.

The critical challenge to society and the agricultural community will be to recognize the need for and benefits of developing, implementing, and supporting policies that work for sustainable agriculture. The support of government must include incentives that encourage sustainable agriculture, as well as opportunities for farmers to achieve success.

Marin County now offers an organic certification program which is accredited by the USDA and verifies compliance with the National Organic Program standards. As of spring, 2006, Marin has 33 registered organic producers farming 2,330 acres, producing food products with a total gross value of almost $4 million. Local organic commodities include apples, beans, berries, broccoli, cabbage, carrots, chard, cucumbers, cut flowers, dairy products, eggs, herbs, and vegetable starts.

Other notable efforts include: zoning regulations that demonstrate a commitment to protecting our agricultural lands; a streamlined permitting process for agricultural operations; the hiring of an Agricultural Ombudsman to help producers meet regulatory requirements; and the development of general land use plans that make specific policy recommendations on sustainability.

Perhaps the most important component is the surrounding community—a community that not only supports agriculture in concept, but is actively supportive of family farms in its shopping practices as well as its politics. 🍃

Elisabeth Ptak

Associate Director, Marin Agricultural Land Trust

More than a year ago, the Wall Street Journal ran an article calling farmers the new celebrities. That theme was echoed at a community dinner in Toby's Feed Barn last fall where one speaker referred to them as rock stars. On the heels of the visit of Prince Charles and the Duchess of Cornwall to that same barn to take in the Point Reyes Farmers' Market a few weeks before, the accolades seemed fitting. Still, I don't imagine most farmers often feel much like big wheels. When I asked one organic vegetable grower how his season had been ("Good!") and what his plans were for next year, he said, "I'm trying to get smarter."

A patchwork quilt made by a Fairfax woman hung from the rafters at one end of the barn, and a bandstand marked the other end. In between, three long rows of tables were set with white linens and wineglasses. If anyone wondered why the barn was so tall, the enormous hay bales stacked almost to the ceiling were the answer. This was a place of busy-ness, but it was also a place of business.

Despite Toby's temporary makeover, the room maintained the feel of authenticity that comes from a tradition of providing for the needs of local farmers and ranchers and a more recent history of going all out for the community. Before the family-style plates of roasted vegetables, cheeses, and meat would be passed around, Nick Giacomini, son of barn owner Chris Giacomini, led us in grace.

A white-haired band from Bolinas began playing while we ate, running through a repertoire that included Cajun music, their own compositions, and tight renditions of Grateful Dead tunes. By dessert time, people had begun to get up from their seats to dance in the small space in front of the musicians. And then, the party was over. We trailed away to our cars and to our homes and to our beds.

The truth is, most rock stars wouldn't have had to get up early the next morning to see that the cows were milked. They wouldn't have been called out in the middle of a rainy winter night to help a ewe struggling to give birth to twin lambs. They wouldn't have had to load a truck with fruits and vegetables to sell at the larger farmers' market in San Rafael now that our local one has closed for the season. But that's where we saw many of the people we had dined with the night before when we did our Thanksgiving shopping on Sunday. Cheerful and busy, the Cinderella celebrities bagged up green beans, arugula, squash, and apples, and counted out our change with the same spirit they'd shown at the party in their honor the night before.

Celebrity is fleeting, and maybe the move to put a face on the farmer will be judged by history to have come too late to save America's farmlands which are disappearing at an alarming rate. But that night, at least, we paid our respects to some of the men and women who grow fruits and vegetables, who raise beef and dairy cows, who farm oysters, make cheese, and nurture flocks of sheep in West Marin. On Sunday, with our purchases, we thanked them again.

MARIN

FARM FAMILIES

STORIES & RECIPES

Mike and Sally Gale's 600-acre ranch in Chileno Valley has been in Sally's family since 1862. Her great-great-grandfather bought the former dairy operation from Henry Halleck, President Abraham Lincoln's Chief of Staff. The ranch now produces grass-fed beef and organic apples.

The Gales had not always intended to be ranchers. They had lived in Hawaii for 20 years when Sally's mother, Anita, deeded the Chileno Valley property to them. It was a wonderful surprise and Mike, Sally, and their three children decided it would be an extraordinary adventure to move back to Marin and renew this family legacy.

"When we took over the ranch in 1995, everything was very seriously dilapidated," says Sally. "The ranch had been abandoned for years, and it was in total disrepair. There was no electricity, no water, and the once stately Victorian farmhouse, built by my great grandfather, was in ruins."

The Gales restored their Victorian farmhouse, built in 1862

It took the Gales five years to restore the home, pastures, fencing, roads, and barns. They even were able to return the creek which runs through the property back to its natural habitat, a major triumph for the family.

"Visitors get an inside look at what a cattle ranch is all about and learn the importance of being responsible stewards of this land."

~ Sally Gale

Sally and Mike feed alfalfa to their Black Angus herd

Today the ranch produces beef from a herd of Black Angus cattle that are born, raised, and processed right on the property. Mike Gale says the family is a bit old-fashioned in the way they raise their beef. And they only sell directly to individuals and families, most of whom live in the Bay Area. "We want people to see where their food comes from, so we keep this entire operation right here," says Mike.

The Gales also raise and sell organic apples and host artist retreats four times a year.

Anita Googens admires her daughter Sally's rose garden

Anita's Veal Stew with Polenta

3–4 lbs. of veal stew meat, coated in flour
3 Tbsp. extra virgin olive oil
3–4 cloves of garlic, chopped
1/2 cup red wine
Pinch each of fresh rosemary, thyme, sage, oregano, and marjoram

Sauté garlic in olive oil in a large frying pan. Add veal that has been coated in flour. Brown meat and add wine and all the herbs. Place all ingredients in a covered cast iron pot. Cook slowly in 275°F oven for 2 hours or until tender.

1 cup polenta
3 cups water
Pinch salt
1 cup grated Monterey jack cheese
Fresh chopped parsley

Stir polenta into water in medium saucepan. Stir constantly over low heat for 40 minutes. Add salt. Remove from stove, and stir in cheese until it is melted. Serve the polenta with the veal on the side. Spoon the gravy from the veal over the top. Garnish with parsley before serving.

The 835-acre Corda Ranch and winery is located in the Chileno Valley between Petaluma and Tomales Bay. The property was purchased in 1927 by the Corda family and began as a dairy operation. The ranch was passed down from generation to generation and is now run by David Corda, his brother Hank, and their mother Minnie.

"Growing up on a dairy farm meant that all the kids, my brother and two sisters, had chores to do," says David. "When I was seven years old, I got up before school started, sometimes before daybreak, to feed the calves. When school was out I came home and cleaned out the stalls."

David says he loved those days. "I always felt good knowing I was taking care of animals. Watching calves being born was a happy time. There was really a lot of joy in being involved with these four-legged families."

Minnie, David's mother, had been raised on a dairy and it was a life she understood and took pride in. "My mom would get up every morning at 1 A.M. to bring the cows in to the milking barn," says David. "Then she would go back to bed and get up again at 6 A.M. to feed the calves and scrub the walls of the barn. She cooked three meals a day and did all the laundry for not only the family, but for the hired men as well. She took care of everybody. During the day, while my dad was doing the heavy work outside, she was working inside. It was a real partnership."

The Cordas *(left to right)*: Hank, Minnie, and David inside their wine cellar

"We are constantly educating the public that all the elements for making a fine wine can be found right here in Marin… Watching a wine drinker discover and enjoy our products is a great part of my job."
~ David Corda

David, his brother Hank, and his parents ran the dairy until 1987. When his father died unexpectedly, the family decided to give up the dairy to concentrate on a beef and silage operation.

"My brother met someone in the wine industry who suggested we expand our operation. He thought we had a great place to grow grapes," says David. "We had a good sloping piece of land in an ideal spot and decided to give it a try."

The Cordas planted their first vines in 1991, and by 1993 they were making wine and selling it to other wineries. The wine was well-regarded, so in 1997 the brothers and Minnie decided to take a leap of faith and launch their own wine-making operation. The Corda Winery was born.

Today, 35 fertile acres are planted in grapes that are producing Pinot Noir, Merlot, Cabernet Franc, and Riesling wines. Last year the company sold 1,500 cases and Corda 1996 Meritage won a prestigious Silver Medal in the *San Francisco Chronicle's* 2001 Wine Competition.

Tasting and testing the wine:
Winemaker Jason Baber & David Corda

"We've got a lot of competition in the wine industry," says David, who often hosts wine tastings around the County.

"We are a young winery competing with the old, established ones in Sonoma and Napa. We are constantly educating the public that all the elements for making a fine wine can be found right here in Marin, and I spend a lot of my time doing just that. Watching a wine drinker discover and enjoy our products is a great part of my job."

The Corda Winery is open to visitors by appointment only.

Corda's Swiss Potato Soup
Courtesy of Ann Corda & *The Corda Family Cookbook*

6 slices thick bacon, cut into 1/2 inch pieces
2 large leeks (white and pale green parts only),
   thinly sliced
2 cups minced onion
3 medium potatoes, pared and cubed

1 large turnip, pared and cubed
6 cups chicken broth
1 cup sour cream
Salt and freshly ground pepper
Chopped parsley

Fry bacon until crisp in Dutch oven. Remove bacon and reserve. Add leeks and onion, sauté covered about 10 minutes until tender. Add potatoes, turnip and chicken broth. Heat to a boil and reduce heat. Simmer covered until all is tender, about 15 minutes. Purée mixture in blender. Return to Dutch oven. Bring to a boil, then remove from heat. Stir in sour cream, add bacon, and season to taste with salt and pepper. Garnish with parsley.

In 1941, German immigrant Bill Straus started a small Marshall dairy with 23 cows, each one named for a friend or family member. Nine years later, Bill and his wife Ellen, both ardent conservationists and strong supporters of sustainable farming methods even before such terms existed, wanted to expand. They leased and later purchased a second ranch on the shores of Tomales Bay.

Today the 660-acre operation is run by their son Albert, who grew up on the farm and converted the dairy to certified organic in 1993. It was the first organic dairy west of the Mississippi. Currently the dairy's 270 Jersey and Holstein cows produce between 3,000 and 4,000 gallons of milk a day. The milk is trucked to the Straus Family Creamery a few miles north of the dairy where it is bottled or processed into organic butter, yogurt, and ice cream.

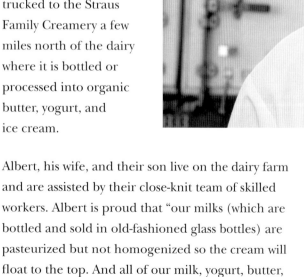

Above: Straus cows grazing
Left: Albert Straus

Albert, his wife, and their son live on the dairy farm and are assisted by their close-knit team of skilled workers. Albert is proud that "our milks (which are bottled and sold in old-fashioned glass bottles) are pasteurized but not homogenized so the cream will float to the top. And all of our milk, yogurt, butter, and ice cream are certified Kosher."

"[An energy system that uses natural gases formed from cow manure] is just one more step towards my goal of having our farm become completely self-sufficient in energy with a minimal impact on the environment."
~ Albert Straus

The Straus Family Creamery bottling operation

The farm uses no pesticides or chemical fertilizers on the land or in the feed. The cows graze the fields from spring through fall and are housed in the open-sided loafing barn during the winter months. When treating sick cows, Albert uses homeopathic medications as much as possible.

Recently, he introduced an environment-ally friendly energy system that uses natural gases formed from cow manure (cows can produce up to 120 lbs. of waste a day) and a "methane digester" to power the operation.

"We like to keep things simple," he continues. "We like making food without added coloring, emulsifier, or additives. We want to keep our products as close to nature as possible. Some of the items we produce are reminiscent of the way we had them as children on the farm or what our parents used to eat in Europe before they immigrated."

"This process could save us up to $6,000 a month in energy costs," he says. "It's just one more step towards my goal of having our farm become completely self-sufficient in energy with a minimal impact on the environment."

Spicy Cheddar Puffs
Makes 50 puffs

1 cup all-purpose flour
1 tsp. ground cumin
1/2 tsp. ground coriander
1/2 tsp. salt
1/2 tsp. freshly ground pepper
1/8 tsp. ground red pepper

1 cup water
6 Tbsp. Straus Salted or Sweet Butter, cut up
4 large eggs
1 cup shredded medium or sharp white cheddar cheese (4 oz.)

1. Heat oven to 400°F. Butter two large cookie sheets. Combine flour, cumin, coriander, salt, pepper, and red pepper in bowl.
2. Bring water and butter to boil in medium saucepan over high heat; boil until butter has melted. Reduce heat to low; add flour mixture all at once. Stir vigorously with wooden spoon until mixture leaves sides of pan and forms a ball.
3. Remove pan from heat. Beat in eggs, one at a time, beating well after each addition, until completely smooth. Stir in cheese.
4. Drop teaspoons of dough on cookie sheets. Bake puffs 25–30 minutes, rotating cookie sheets halfway through baking, until golden. Transfer to wire racks. Serve warm or at room temperature.

Hog Island Oyster Company

John Finger, Terry Sawyer, Michael Watchorn

In the mid-1980s, three marine biologists came up with an idea that would change their lives forever. John Finger, Michael Watchorn, and Terry Sawyer joined forces to create a little piece of aquatic history on Tomales Bay: the Hog Island Oyster Company.

Located in the tiny town of Marshall, today the operation leases 135 off-shore acres from the State Department of Fish and Game and produces more than two million prized oysters a year. The oysters start out as small seeds, "no bigger than a grain of granola," says Sawyer. The tiny bivalves are as carefully tended as nursery plants, then are put into the bay and moved from location to location until they reach maturity. It takes from one to two years to create a prime Hog Island oyster.

"We coax our oysters to grow in a round shell and keep them separate from one another, as that is critical for the delicate flavor and texture that we are looking for," says Sawyer. "By the time our oysters are mature and ready for the market, they've been practically hand-raised and gone from their nursery environment into our carefully monitored tidal water beds."

The partners purchase their seedlings in lots of 100,000–500,000 from trusted, prime hatcheries who know the kind of product the company wants to produce. The oysters are cultivated in a variety of closely watched micro-climates, harvested, sorted, and sold right from the aquaculture farm in Marshall—between 40,000 and 50,000 oysters every single week of the year.

John Finger at the oyster farm on Tomales Bay

"To protect this incredible agricultural resource we all have in Marin County, we must have minimal impact, both on the land and in the water." ~ Terry Sawyer

Four different species with marked characteristics are produced: Atlantic; Kumomoto; European Flat; and the company's most popular, Sweetwater. In addition to oysters, the company also grows and sells clams and mussels.

"Everything we do here is towards sustainability and becoming observant stewards of what we have," says Sawyer. "Our farming practices have a critical impact on the planet. To protect this incredible agricultural resource we all have in Marin County, we must have minimal impact, both on the land and in the water. I think this is the goal of almost every single grower and rancher in West Marin."

Oysters are harvested by boat

The company, which has 17 employees at its Marshall location, also owns the wildly-popular restaurant Hog Island Oyster Oyster Company bar and restaurant at the Ferry Building in San Francisco and a catering company that has delivered, presented, and shucked up to 10,000 oysters—for one event at a local winery—that were consumed in less than three hours! 🍃

Hog Island oysters are sold at the farm in Marshall and at the San Francisco Ferry Building

Hogwash

**Hog Island Oyster Company's
Signature Dipping Sauce For Fresh Oysters**

1/4 **cup seasoned rice vinegar**
1/4 **cup natural rice vinegar**
1 **large shallot, peeled and chopped fine**
1 **jalapeno pepper, seeded and chopped fine**
1/2 **bunch of cilantro, washed and chopped fine**
Juice from 1 lime

Combine ingredients, chill, and serve with fresh Hog Island oysters.

Terry Sawyer shucks oysters with his wife Laurie at "Taste of Marin" which is held annually and co-sponsored by Marin Agricultural Land Trust and Marin Organic   *Photo: Elisabeth Ptak*

David Little grew up in San Anselmo, where he began work in the family business as a third-generation Marin roofer. He learned about farming when he helped a friend run his ranch near Tomales. When his friend passed away, David and his family moved onto the property to take care of it. Suddenly, he knew something in his life had changed. Roofing just wasn't going to do it for him anymore. David wanted to be a farmer.

The land around the ranch had a history of being ideal for growing potatoes so that's what David decided to grow. It was economically feasible because the investment was manageable (potatoes can be planted for about $1,000 an acre compared to strawberries which will run about $6,000 an acre or grapes which will cost about $10,000 an acre). Since he was starting from scratch and potatoes don't require huge amounts of water or equipment, it was an ideal way to begin his new venture.

Still, David's first year, 1995, was a tough one. Tractors got stuck, engines blew up, but David persevered. He loved the smell of the earth and the process of creating life from a seed. A little machinery challenge didn't get him down. He borrowed equipment and figured out the process as he went along.

David Little (*in back*) and employee Cleto Gurrola harvest potatoes by hand
Below: David rides the tractor with pal Dot

"I really love being a farmer. There are just all these little magical things that happen that aren't going to occur many other places."

~ David Little

"I knew I was officially in business when I actually purchased my first tractor. That was a great day," says David. "And I really love being a farmer. There are just all these little magical things that happen that aren't going to occur many other places.

"Not long ago, I was on my tractor and looked down to see this wonderful covey of quails—the little babies just following so close to their parents. I had to stop and watch. Suddenly a huge hawk flew out of the sky and started hovering, ready for a kill. I couldn't decide if I should intervene with nature and pull up my blade to scare the hawk or just let things take their course. Just when I couldn't hold out any longer, two swallows zoomed in like gunfire and began pecking at the hawk. The hawk flew back into the sky, and my little family of quail got to go on with the business of living. Now, how much better can you get than that?"

Little Organic Farm grows a variety of select organic potatoes (German Butterballs are the current best seller) as well as onions, strawberries, Jerusalem artichokes, squash, and dry-farmed tomatoes.

David and his wife Beverly at the Marin County Farmers Market

Pouch Potatoes

2 organic yellow flesh potatoes
1 organic sweet onion, chopped
2 organic cloves garlic, minced

3 Tbsp. olive oil
Salt and pepper to taste
16 inches of aluminum foil

Cut potatoes into wedges and put in a bowl. Add chopped onion, garlic, olive oil, salt and pepper. Mix all ingredients together and put into center of the foil. Close the foil up and put it on the grill for 20 minutes until done.

Dry Farm Early Girl Tomato Spread

12 or more organic Early Girl tomatoes
4 Tbsp. olive oil

3 cloves organic garlic, minced
Salt and pepper to taste

Place tomatoes stem side down and close together on a cookie sheet. Drizzle on top: olive oil, minced garlic, salt, and pepper. Turn oven to lowest heat about, 200°F. David Little says, "Go to bed. When you get up in the morning, take your squished tomatoes out of the oven, puree them and use in sauces, salsas, soups, what have you. You will not believe the flavor and it freezes well."

Located at the mouth of Walker Creek, the 1,125-acre Pozzi Ranch has the kind of natural beauty that can take your breath away. Wildflowers carpet hillsides that ease down to Tomales Bay. Pelicans and cormorants soar above the rolling hills. Hog Island looks close enough to touch. The property also has a vivid human history. Site of a commercial wharf in the mid-19th century, the ranch's Preston's Point once boasted a store, a warehouse, a dance hall, even a caged bear. Today, that spit of land and the surrounding acreage have reverted to bucolic pasture where sheep and cattle graze.

Sally and Marin Pozzi with Regina and Steven

Owners Sally and Martin Pozzi leased the property for four years before purchasing it in the summer of 2005. Both Martin and Sally Pozzi were born and raised in farming families. Sally's southern California family has grown citrus and avocado crops for five generations. Martin's great grandparents settled in Occidental in 1880, and he grew up just one half mile away from his current ranch on his family's home place in Tomales—150 acres purchased in 1915, where they ran a dairy and, later, a beef and sheep operation.

The Pozzis have two children, and the ranching life is a big part of their upbringing, just as it was for their parents. "Because our children work with us," Sally says, "they learn about life cycles, the laws of nature, and how things work. They know how to raise animals, how to feed and care for them, how animals are born, that the birthing process includes risk, how and why we need to vaccinate, how to drive a vehicle, how to make the water work and that, if we have to, we can survive without electricity."

"Because our children work with us, they learn about life cycles, the laws of nature, and how things work." ~ Sally Pozzi

Like a lot of seven-year-old boys, Steven Pozzi builds trucks from Lego® blocks. But on Steven's vehicles, the yellow blocks become bales of hay. He also imagines a tractor, a real one, and describes how he'd use it to cut thistles, scrape the ranch roads, and herd sheep. Regina, nine years old, loves to read. She's also in 4-H, and she showed the calf and lambs she's raising for the first time at the county fair last year.

In fact, their parents say that the Pozzi children are actively involved in everything having to do with the ranch, whether it's fixing fences, delivering hay, or attending meetings of the Marin County Board of Supervisors when agricultural issues are being discussed. Sally serves as president of the Marin County Farm Bureau, and Martin is a past president.

In addition to their active family farm business, they advocate for agricultural issues at the local, state, and federal levels.

"We need to keep agriculture healthy and viable," Sally says. "Our children know there is a financial aspect to ranching, and that the lambs and calves are sold in late spring, and we receive one check for them each year. They understand the ranching income is marginal and always fluctuating; they have seen the calves auctioned."

When it's shearing time, the kids are up at daybreak, helping to sort the animals, even though the market for sheep's wool is so bad that Martin says he gives it away. "Recently, we've received a fair price for the meat. We supplement that income with our beef herd and our hay business."

If succeeding in agriculture today means knitting together a combination of businesses, the Pozzis are willing to do it. "We've done a lot to survive," Sally says. "We're not afraid to try things."

Regina and Steven with their sheep and rabbit

Fran's Fruit Cobbler

"My mother was known as a fantastic cook and her cobblers sold at various auctions and fundraisers for hundreds of dollars. This easy recipe has few ingredients and is difficult to mess up. She was most famous for making blackberry cobbler but also made, peach, apricot, boysenberry, ollalieberry, raspberry, apple, and various combinations." ~Sally Pozzi

Fruit of choice, sweetened　　　**3 Tbsp. flour**
1/4 pound butter　　　　　　　**1/2 tsp. baking powder**
1 cup sugar　　　　　　　　　　**1/4 cup or so warm milk**
3/4 cup flour

Put sweetened fruit in a **9 x 9** in. baking pan. Melt butter and combine with 1 cup sugar and 3/4 cup flour. Remove one cup of mixture and set aside. To remainder, add the 3 Tbsp. flour, 1/2 tsp. baking powder, and warm milk to make a thick batter. Pour batter over fruit, crumble mixture over top and sprinkle cinnamon to taste. Bake at 350° for one hour.

Pozzi story and family photo:
Elisabeth Ptak
Photo this page: Sally Pozzi

The 700-acre Box A Ranch runs along both sides of the Shoreline Highway in Tomales at the northernmost tip of Marin County. Originally a dairy ranch, today the property is a beef and sheep operation run by Al Poncia and his 85-year-old mother Jennie.

The business has been in the family for more than a century. The original home ranch was purchased in 1901 by Al's grandfather Angelo. When Al's parents—Al, Sr. and Jennie—were married in 1938, they took over a second ranch that had been purchased previously by Angelo and began the 35-cow dairy operation where Al grew up.

In those days, his parents would milk the cows by hand twice a day. When he was just an infant, Al's mother would bundle him up in a papoose, hang it from the barn wall, and milk the cows under the fascinated eyes of her baby boy.

Jennie, a widow for almost 30 years, continues to play a pivotal part in the history of the Poncia family. She lives nearby in the original farmhouse and continues to drive the tractor and shepherd her own herd of sheep. She walks the hills every day, her gardens

Ranchwoman Jenny Poncia   *Photo: Cathie Poncia*

"Everyday it is different and beautiful… I love the work ethic that has made this whole agricultural community so strong. This is where I belong."   ~ Al Poncia

are bountiful, and her affinity for all creatures great and small is evident. Every night she prepares a mayonnaise and baloney sandwich for her dog Jay, who she found alone and shivering in the cold outdoors 12 years ago. Now, where is any pooch going to get that kind of service?

"She is extraordinary," says Cathie Poncia, Al's wife. "I've never known anyone who has worked as hard as Jennie. Her love for nature and her contributions in our community are unmatched."

The Poncias pasture their animals—220 cows and 100 sheep—in several different fields and work hard with family and friends to protect and restore creek beds and riparian areas.

Poncia Dairy, 1920   *Photo courtesty of the Poncia Family*

When Al was growing up, he had lots of farm chores, but his parents wanted him to have a life without having to do all the hard work they had to do during the depression years. A friend of his told him, "Don't ever learn how to milk cows because once you do, you'll be stuck forever!" So Al deferred actually working fulltime on the dairy until after he completed his education.

In the late 1960s, Al wasn't sure if he could make it financially and began selling insurance to make ends meet. When the 1967 draft of the Countywide General Plan proposed subdivision of agricultural land, shopping centers, housing developments, and a city of 150,000 on the shores of Tomales Bay, Al and many other ranchers joined forces with conservationists to fight those changes. Thanks to their efforts, West Marin remains the agricultural heart of the County.

Cathie & Al Poncia celebrate their anniversary at "Wedding Rock" overlooking their ranch

Asked who his mentor has been, Al is emphatic. "[The late Olema rancher] Boyd Stewart was my greatest teacher. I'm a little rebel, and he taught me to listen and never shut a door. He told me I could fight like the devil, but those same people I was fighting might become some of my greatest supporters. He said even if folks were 180 degrees apart philosophically, we could still respect one another. He was an amazing man."

One of the things Al loves most about his life is waking up and going to the kitchen table to look out the big picture window at the amazing panorama before him. "Everyday it is different and beautiful," he says. "This is the only life I've known. I love the work ethic that has made this whole agricultural community so strong. This is where I belong." 🖋

Veal in Wine & Cheese Sauce Bedded on Noodles

1 1/2 lbs. veal stew meat
2 Tbsp. olive oil
1 clove garlic, finely chopped
1/2 tsp. mixed Italian Seasonings
1 tsp. salt
1/2 cup + 1/3 cup Sauterne wine (may substitute a dry white wine such as Sauvignon Blanc)
2 cups flat noodles (cooked according to pkg. directions)

2 Tbsp. butter
1 1/2 Tbsp. flour
1 1/4 cup milk
3/4 tsp. salt
1/4 cup grated parmesan cheese (plus additional to sprinkle over the dish)
Dash of paprika

Dice veal and brown slowly in oil. Add garlic and herbs and sauté a minute longer. Stir in 1/2 cup wine and salt. Cover and simmer for 45 minutes. Melt butter in saucepan over low heat. Stir in flour and cook until integrated. Stir in milk and salt and cook until thick. Stir in cheese and remaining 1/3 cup wine. Mix 3/4 of the cheese sauce with noodles and place in 9 x 13 in. baking dish. Place meat on top of noodles and pour remaining cheese sauce on top. Sprinkle with parmesan and paprika. Bake at 350°F for 25–30 minutes.

Members of David Evans' family have been ranching in the County since his Swiss grandfather immigrated to West Marin in 1889. Today David and his parents Dan and Dolores own or lease 3,800 acres of pastureland in West Marin. More than 2,000 acres are certified organic.

In 1999 David launched Marin Sun Farms, his grass-fed beef and pasture-raised chicken operation. "The overwhelming demand for our products is growing at an incredible rate," says David. "We are producing 60 dozen eggs a day and are processing seven heads of cattle a week. I started with just a handful of workers, and now I am managing 25 employees."

David comes from a traditional cattle and livestock family and is breaking new ground in his family by adopting organic certification and techniques.

"Our chickens live in a pasture and eat a natural diet," David says, adding that the "eggs hit the market two days after being laid." All of his animals roam free and are never treated with hormones, antibiotics, or rendered animal protein. "We stay away from all additives or feed that is strictly for fattening the animals. I want to keep our environment and food supply totally in balance."

David Evans in front of his Point Reyes Station butcher shop and eatery. The operation was closed temporarily due to winter storm damage, but will reopen summer, 2006.

"I want to make the land productive for generations to come and create a food system that supports our community."

~ David Evans

David's goal is sustainability. "I want to make the land productive for generations to come and create a food system that supports our community. My passion is to grow, produce. and buy locally. Many are resisting change, but all of us need to address our relationship with nature, with sustainability, and embrace it without a struggle."

When David gets requests for his beef from the east coast, he turns them down. "I suggest they find a respected local producer for their needs. I am an idealist and feel strongly about how we grow our food, feed our animals, nurture our land. The biggest joy for me is walking down the street and being stopped by someone who has just eaten and loves what I produce. That's the joy about being local and it's about as far from Foster Farms as it's going to get."

Marin Sun Farms grass-fed beef cows graze in a scenic pasture above the Nicasio Reservoir
Photo: Dexter Roberts

Beef Goulash

1 Tbsp. caraway seeds	**1 tsp. minced fresh thyme**
2 Tbsp. olive oil	**1 bay leaf**
2 large onions, thinly sliced	**3 Tbsp. tomato paste**
1 Tbsp. sugar	**4 cups chicken stock**
3 garlic cloves, minced	**2 1/2 lbs. trimmed Marin Sun Farms boneless**
2 Tbsp. minced fresh marjoram	**chuck, cut into 2 inch pieces**
1 Tbsp. paprika*	**Salt and freshly ground pepper**

1. In a small skillet, toast the caraway seeds over moderate heat until darkened and fragrant, about 1 minute. Transfer the caraway to a spice grinder and let cool completely. Grind into a powder.
2. Heat the olive oil in a large enameled cast-iron casserole. Add the sliced onions and sugar and cook over moderate heat, stirring occasionally, until the onions are evenly golden, about 20 minutes. Add the minced garlic and ground caraway to the casserole and cook, stirring, for 1 minute. Add the paprika, marjoram, thyme, and bay leaf and cook, stirring, about 2 minutes. Stir in the tomato paste and then the chicken stock. Add the meat, season with salt and pepper, and simmer on stovetop or in moderate oven (about 250° F) until the meat is very tender—about 2 hours. Skim off the fat, add pepper if necessary, and serve.

* Recommended: fresh dried paprika from Tierra Vegetables of Santa Rosa (available in late autumn) or substitute sweet Hungarian paprika.

Based on a recipe in Food & Wine *Magazine's 2002 Cookbook*

Allstar Organics began 11 years ago when Marty Jacobsen and Janet Brown first grew organic tomatoes for their family on the terraced hillside of their Lagunitas home. They gradually expanded the garden over two acres.

"Organic farming was Janet's calling," says Marty. "For me, the whole thing just evolved. It wasn't something I dreamed about for years, but the more I learned, the more I loved the whole process. Now it's as vital to me as it is to Janet."

If they were going to make this dream really work, they decided they needed more land than the acreage around their home. When Randy Lafranchi, a fourth-generation dairyman, offered the couple the opportunity to farm a fertile eight-acre plot of land in Nicasio, they jumped at the opportunity.

Today Allstar Organics is located on a rich, flat piece of property in the heart of Nicasio. The farm has become well-known and popular for its organic produce and, in particular, for heirloom tomatoes.

"We are growing about 50 different tomatoes, each with its own very distinct and subtle characteristics," says Janet. "Our heirlooms come from seeds that sometimes have passed through four generations of growers. They flourish because we know how to take care of them. They are thin-skinned and love this weather. The cool, moist nights and warm days are perfect for the slow-ripening process that they need to develop their full flavor and texture. I like to think that our tomatoes are cozy in this inland, Marin County field."

Janet, Marty, and their crew of knowledgeable workers know exactly when the heirloom tomatoes must be

Janet and Marty with their sunflower crop

"When [heirlooms] are harvested at their peak, they retain the complex, tremendously sweet flavors of old-fashioned garden tomatoes." ~ Janet Brown

picked. "You need to use a sensory awareness when you're in the field," says Janet. "We select varieties that are vivid and dazzling in character. When they are harvested at their peak, they retain the complex, tremendously sweet flavors of old-fashioned garden tomatoes."

Marty says that sometimes there are challenges in this kind of farming. "There was one especially large plant that had one exceptionally beautiful tomato growing on it. I became intrigued with this one tomato and for three months, would follow its growth. Everyday I was out there looking at this unbelievable tomato and I was getting really excited because I knew it would produce great seeds. On the day it was ready to pick, I ran out there to get my prize and I couldn't believe it. It was gone! A gopher had eaten my tomato!"

Woodlands Market in Kentfield was Allstar's first important commercial customer. "They loved our tomatoes and bought as much as we grew," says Marty. "They encouraged us to diversify beyond

Marty grows 50 squash varieties

tomatoes, so we soon began growing heirloom varieties of everything from basil, squash, and pumpkins to eggplant, peppers, and melons."

By February 2004, when Allstar had quadrupled its production, another project turned from a pastime into a full-time avocation. Janet had become an enthusiastic grower of heirloom roses. She started with a few varieties and now cultivates more than 400 antique perfume roses in 50 different varieties, all grown organically on the couple's Lagunitas property.

"We began to explore the possibility of distilling our rose petals in order to create authentic organic rose water," says Janet. "We focused on consistency and within a few years achieved a high-quality product that is steam-distilled and contains no chemicals, preservatives, or alcohol. Now we are producing six hydrosols and essential oils which include everything from rosemary and lavender to bay laurel and California coastal sage." Called "Landscape," this line of organic and locally produced essentials oils and floral waters is now a solid part of the growing Allstar family farm.

Organic Heirloom Tomato Caviar

2 cups dried organic *heirloom* tomatoes*
3–5 cloves organic garlic
Organic extra virgin olive oil
Reggiano Parmesan cheese

Chop dried tomatoes into small pieces. Put 1/2 cup tomatoes, one clove of garlic, and a few tablespoons of olive oil into food processor. Pulse until tomatoes are finely chopped. Add a thinly sliced piece of Parmesan cheese and pulse again. Continue to add more tomatoes, oil, garlic and cheese until a thick crimson paste is formed. Serve with homemade crackers. Also good as a pizza topping or stirred into fresh, hot pasta.

*If not available, use the best dried organic tomatoes you can find. Do not use non-organic dried tomatoes, or dried tomatoes packed in oil.

Liz and Bruce Daniels raise grass-fed Angus beef cows

Liz and Bruce Daniels raise Black Angus and Texas Longhorn cows on their 500-acre ranch in Nicasio. The couple bought the former dairy 19 years ago. Today they nurture 140 grass-fed and hormone and antibiotic-free cows there.

"Our Longhorn operation is unique because most people don't know what a fine beef they produce. They are magical to me because they are so hearty and compact and give birth so easily," says Liz.

Bruce, a full-time large animal veterinarian, manages the beef operation. Liz manages everything else—from her two-acre certified organic market garden to her own company for which she designs and manufactures everything from baby clothes and aprons to sachets and home-made vinegars.

"We work together well. We built our barn from scratch, put in plumbing, and designed and constructed our greenhouse."
~ Liz Daniels

Liz grows lavender and other organic crops

"It's a wonderful life on this ranch because we are busy all the time. And for me, it's a great workout, because when I'm not walking all around the property, helping with round-ups or tending to the cattle, I'm gardening, weed-whacking, or mowing!"

The greatest influence in Liz's life is her husband. "He's a full-time vet and a full-time rancher and has figured out how to make it all balance. We work together well. We built our barn from scratch, put in plumbing, and designed and constructed our greenhouse. We've done a pretty good job raising our now-grown daughter together, and I would say we are a darn good team."

Although Liz was raised in San Francisco and still fancies the city life once in a while, her heart is in the country. "My grandfather was a rancher, and I grew up loving horses. I rode and trained polo ponies in Texas and taught and trained horses in West Marin for more than 20 years."

The horse barn was built in 1871, five years after Custer's last stand

Lavender Shortbread

1 1/2 cup cornstarch	2 1/4 cup butter
1 1/2 cup powdered sugar	1/3 cup organic lavender (can
3 cups sifted flour	crush in a clean coffee grinder)

Mix all ingredients together and bake in 8 x 8 inch pan for 20 minutes at 320°F.

Pumpkin Soup

6 cups peeled and de-seeded cooked, chopped organic pumpkin

3 cups scalded milk

Mix pumpkin and milk together and add:

1 Tbsp. butter	Salt and pepper
1 Tbsp. white sugar or	Pinch each of nutmeg,
2 Tbsp. brown sugar	cinnamon and saffron

Heat, but not to boiling, and serve at once.

Wind Tryst Ranch has been in the Tomasini family over a century. Today, it is an active 500-acre beef operation run by Heloise Tomasini with help from her grown children and trusted ranch hands.

When Heloise married Henry Tomasini, he was a prominent Petaluma banker with a penchant for wearing beautifully cut suits. But behind his pin-striped image, a cowboy in overalls was waiting to get out and run a ranch.

As a young married couple, Heloise and her husband leased a ranch outside Stockton. When Wind Tryst Ranch in Nicasio was deeded to Henry by his mother, he and Heloise and their four children decided to move onto the long-neglected property, even though the old abandoned farmhouse had no insulation and few modern conveniences. While Henry commuted to his banking operation, Heloise raised their children and learned the ropes of managing a cattle operation.

Heloise on her patio festooned with her giant begonias

"We wanted to run a profitable business," says Heloise, "so we bought very fine registered cows for breeding purposes. My husband spent weekends doing everything from branding and vaccinating to fixing fences and maintaining our herd."

The weekends were wonderful family times and all of the children worked with their dad on the ranch. "He was an only child," says Eloise, "and he loved this family time with our children. The kids thrived in this environment, were all active in 4-H, and were driving tractors before they were seven years old."

The Tomasinis had an active social life, but nothing came before taking care of the cattle. "I had just had my hair done and was dressed to the nines for a dinner party being given by some friends," remembers Heloise. "It was pouring rain and there was an emergency with one of the cows. I grabbed my boots and ran out into the night only to get stuck in the wettest pile of mud and manure you could image. My boots were sucked off, my hair was in shambles, but the job had to be done. It's just a way of life for anybody who is running a hands-on cattle operation."

On his retirement from his banking profession in 1984, Henry became a full-time rancher. When he passed away ten years later, Heloise continued the legacy. She has a truck filled with bales of hay, she checks on the care and feeding of her cattle, and she goes on round-ups twice a year. Her life is full and she wouldn't have it any other way. ✒

Friendly, Jr. and his gals are on alert for Heloise's familiar truck

> *"The kids thrived in this environment, were all active in 4-H, and were driving tractors before they were seven years old."*
>
> ~ Heloise Tomasini

Joe's Special

1 onion, chopped
2 cloves of garlic, chopped
2 Tbsp. olive oil
1 lb. ground beef
1 pkg. chopped frozen spinach, thawed and drained well
3 eggs, beaten
Sage, thyme, oregano, salt, and pepper to taste
1/2 lb. sliced mushrooms
1 Tbsp. butter

Sauté onion and garlic in olive oil until softened. Add ground meat and brown. Combine spinach, herbs, spices, and the beaten eggs. Add to meat mixture and stir until firm. In separate pan, sauté mushrooms in butter. Place over meat mixture before serving.

Wind Tryst's highest hill is certainly windy as Heloise exits her Scout

Friendly, Jr. greets Heloise

Nan Tucker McEvoy didn't originally intend to recreate a Tuscan olive grove in West Marin. She was merely looking for a "wonderful place in the country where my three grandchildren could experience the great outdoors." But when she learned the 550-acre-ranch she had fallen in love with was zoned for agriculture, she had to decide what kind of crop she would raise.

Nan had grown up loving olive oil and remembers lugging countless bottles back from her travels to Italy. After reading *Feast of the Olive* by Bay Area chef Maggie Klein, she became enchanted with the olive oil-making process. That's when she decided that making an extra virgin olive oil was exactly what she was going to do with her land.

In 1991 Nan hired Maurizio Castelli, one of Tuscany's top experts on the production of olive oil. He was instrumental in importing and planting the first 1,000 olive trees which included six Italian varietals including Frantoio, Leccino, Pendolino, Maurino,

Nan Tucker McEvoy with her olive groves in the background

Shari DeJoseph, Orchard Manager, checks the olives

I was merely looking for a "wonderful place in the country where my three grandchildren could experience the great outdoors."
~ Nan Tucker McEvoy

Leccio del Corno, and Cortina. Maurizio suggested that if they were going to make the best olive oil, they would need the best mill. It wasn't long before a state-of-the-art frantoio, the press used to crush the olives, was ordered. Within months it was ready to produce what today has become McEvoy's prize-winning extra virgin olive oil.

Today the ranch boasts 18,000 olive trees spread over eighty acres. The olives are picked in the fall and crushed on the premises within days of the harvest. Approximately 150 tons of olives are crushed and pressed each harvest season, yielding approximately 4,500 gallons of extra virgin olive oil. In addition, the ranch produces a line of olive oil-based soaps, fruit conserves, and honey.

Sergio Tolentino, orchard truck driver, loads the olive harvest

Netting placed on the ground catches the olives when harvested

Olio Nuovo and Lemon Cookies

Makes approximately 5 dozen cookies. Preheat oven to 350°F.

2 cups unbleached flour
1 cup sugar

1/2 tsp. baking soda

Sift dry ingredients together in a medium bowl.

3/4 cup McEvoy Ranch Certified
  Organic *Olio Nuovo*
4 tsp. lemon zest, grated

1/8 tsp. pure lemon oil such as
  Boyajian brand
1 tsp. lemon juice

Stir liquid ingredients together. Add to dry ingredients until mixture comes together into a uniform mass. Roll dough into 3/4–1 inch balls. Place balls two inches apart on two parchment paper-lined baking sheets. Bake one sheet at a time for 15 minutes or until cooked through and lightly browned.

Lemon and Olive Oil Sorbet

Makes approximately 1½ quarts

1 3/4 cups water

1 1/2 cups sugar

Heat water and sugar in saucepan until sugar is dissolved. Set aside to cool.

1 3/4 cups lemon juice
1 1/4 cups McEvoy Ranch Certified
  Organic Extra Virgin Olive Oil

1 egg white
1 tsp. lemon zest, grated

Add remaining ingredients to sugar solution and whisk well to combine. Place mixture in ice cream freezer and process following manufacturers instructions.

Recipes © Gerald Gass, Ranch Chef

*Photo of Nan,
courtesy McEvoy Ranch*

Jim Grossi and his ten siblings were raised on the farmland where he still lives, just two miles west of Novato. Now in his mid-nineties, Jim remembers that, "From the time we were six years old, we worked on the farm. Each one of us had a string of cows that we were responsible for milking and that's the first thing we did every single morning. After that was done we would clean out the barn and give our cows their feed. When we got home from school, we would do the same thing all over again."

Milking their animals by hand, the children worked until they had filled a five-gallon bucket. As they got older, the youngsters would be responsible for more and more cows. By the time Jim was 13 years old, he was helping with the fencing, cutting and baling hay, and tending his 15 cows every day of the week.

Jim Grossi, Sr. in his apple orchard

Grossi family, 1920. Jim, Sr. is second from right

Photo courtesy Jim Grossi

There are more than 180 Grossi ranching relatives working on dairies or beef operations in Marin County

The Grossi children all attended a one-room school house with youngsters of every age and skill level. There was just one teacher, and she always had her hands full. One of those teachers, Miss Redding, would ride her horse over the hills from her house in Nicasio to the one-room schoolhouse in Novato near Stafford Lake. She did this every single school day, regardless of the rain, winds, and bad weather she encountered.

Jim's father continued to acquire more ranches and eventually owned more than 6,000 acres in Marin. With his children, he ran seven separate dairy operations. Jim loved the life of a dairyman, and never had any interest in working for someone else to get a paycheck. His beloved wife Rose has passed away, and his four children are grown and working in various careers.

Today, replacement dairy heifers and beef cattle are raised on this particular Grossi Ranch, and Jim estimates that there are more than

180 ranching relatives working on other dairies or beef operations in Marin County.

Jim loves animals, and his constant companion is Joey, a big black cat who "understands my English and is a great friend." Some time back, he had another companion, Croakie the wild turkey. "Croakie lived on the roof and when she got hungry, I'd let her in the house and feed her some crackers. She loved sleeping on the roof, and I certainly missed her when she ran into some bad luck with the raccoons." Jim also still misses his best buddy Sparky, the black-and-white fox terrier who followed him everywhere for 17 years.

Now retired, Jim spends much of his time in his small orchard picking the fruit and making, according to those who have tasted it, some of the best applesauce in the county. 🌿

Jim, Sr. with his son Jim, who lives nearby

Jim Grossi's Applesauce

Pick some very good apples (Pippins are best). Peel and core them. Slice them and put them in a large pot. Add a small amount of water to cover and cook very slowly for about two hours. Add more water if too thick. Add a little bit of cinnamon but no sugar unless apples are really tart. When cool, spoon into jars and keep in the refrigerator. Enjoy!

Mamma Grossi's Bread Soup

This 80-year-old recipe was created by Jim's mother. He says it tastes like gruel but he makes it to this day and still enjoys it.

Break up some stale French bread and put it into a pot of boiling water. Add salt to taste and cook until the bread is soft. Add a little butter before serving.

Situated within the Golden Gate National Recreation Area in Olema, the 1,900-acre Stewart Ranch, an Angus beef cattle operation, is run by JoAnn Stewart and her daughter, Amanda Wisby. The sprawling ranch, a dairy until 1972, has been operated by both male and female family members since it was acquired by the Stewart family in 1924.

"My father rode horses and worked on the ranch until he was in his nineties," says JoAnn, daughter of legendary West Marin cattleman, Boyd Stewart.

"Now my daughter Amanda, who has been involved in the cattle business almost all her life, has taken over the reins and is carrying on the Stewart tradition for the fourth generation."

Amanda and her husband K.C. Campbell work seven days a week tending to their 200 certified Angus beef cows, a horse boarding facility, and an organic chicken farm. They live in an 1864 farm house with their seven-year-old son, Stewart.

"You think you run the ranch but the truth is, the livestock runs you!" says Amanda, a 1990 graduate of Dominican University. "We've got 25 registered Morgan horses and everything we do is on horseback. My son was with me in the saddle to gather the cows when he was less than two months old. Having a new baby doesn't get you out of the work that has to be done."

Amanda and K.C. with their son Stewart, his horse, and heifer

Left: The Tack Room

"We've got 25 registered Morgan horses and everything we do is on horseback. My son was with me in the saddle to gather the cows when he was less than two months old."

~ Amanda Wisby

Amanda, who has a small, highly-regarded organic egg business, is up at dawn to "feed the cows, horses, and chickens, then let them all out so we can clean the barns and the pens and take care of daily business. There's not a dull moment."

She says the best part of this life is that she can honestly say she has never been bored one single day in her life and gives high praise to her heroes, the veterinarians, whose dedication and skill have helped to make the ranch such a success.

To her son Stewart, the best part of being a rancher is doing the farm work and making money for doing it. "I once had this calf named Richard," he says. "He was black and he followed me everywhere I went except to school. And at school I missed him. I'd come home and feed him and one day a mother cow lost her baby and she took Richard as her son and I thought that was nice."

Boyd Stewart with daughter JoAnn, granddaughter Amanda, and great grandson Stewart in 2000
Photo © Art Rogers, Pt. Reyes

Very Apple Pie

10 inch pie plate with 2–3 inch sides	I tsp. salt
2 cups sifted flour	3/4 cup **Crisco** shortening
	4–5 Tbsp. ice cold water

Combine flour and salt. Using a pastry blender, cut in the shortening until coarse crumbs form. Sprinkle ice water over pastry while mixing with fork until dough forms. Place dough on wax paper or cutting board that has been sprinkled with flour. Roll out with rolling pin to fit 10-inch pie plate. Using a fork, puncture holes in bottom and sides of crust. Bake in 350°F oven for 30–45 minutes or until golden brown.

8 medium to large apples, peeled & sliced	2 Tbsp. flour
I Tbsp. lemon juice,	1/4 tsp. ground nutmeg
1/2 cup white sugar	1/2 tsp. ground cinnamon
1/2 cup brown sugar	1/2 tsp. salt
	2 Tbsp. cold butter, crumbled

Mix apples with all ingredients. Layer in the baked pie shell, forming a pyramid shape. Place pie on baking pan in 400°F oven for 20 minutes. Reduce heat to 325°F and continue baking for 20 minutes. Serve warm.

Warren Weber, owner of Star Route Farms in Bolinas, began with five acres, horse-drawn sulky plows, cultivators, and a lot of what he calls "long-haired ambition." An organic farming pioneer, he started his business in 1974, making Star Route the oldest certified organic farm in California.

Warren didn't begin life as a farmer. Born in the Midwest and schooled on the east coast, he was a secondary school teacher, then moved to Berkeley to get his Ph.D. A growing dissatisfaction with city life led him to the "Back to the Land" movement in the late 1960s.

"I had worked on ranches as a kid growing up and always felt more at home in the country than in the city," says Warren. "I was part of that hippie culture and decided to live as simply I could, and grow my own food on a piece of land I bought in Bolinas."

He lived there without running water and electricity for a number of years. Oldtimers considered him "likeable, but a bit strange," he recalls. Today the 40-acre certified organic farm produces a rich variety of cool weather vegetables, fruits, and leafy greens.

Warren Weber at his Bolinas farm

Below: Agostino Torres (*foreground*) and Luis Zamora picking crops

"It is very satisfying to be growing wonderful, tasty fruits and vegetables that are in harmony with nature, are good for the planet, and are held in such high regard by the consumer," says Warren. He gives much credit for the quality of his produce to farm manager Doug Gallagher, Annabelle Lenderink, his marketing whiz, and the "fine men and women employed in our fields, offices, and delivery trucks who want everyone to be as satisfied as we are."

Favorite Arugula Salad
Serves 4

1/4 cup champagne or white balsamic vinegar
1/2 cup imported walnut oil
8 cups arugula, washed and spun dry
  (about 8 large handfuls)
1 ripe comice pear, peeled and diced
1/2 cup chopped walnuts, toasted and cooled

Whisk together vinegar and oil. Set aside. In a large salad bowl, combine arugula, pear, and walnuts. Drizzle vinaigrette overall. Toss gently. Serve immediately.

A Simple Orange & Fennel Salad

2 oranges
1 bulb fennel
3 Tbsp. olive oil
Pinch of coarse-ground black pepper
Optional: 2 Tbsp. almonds, toasted and/or
  4 oz. smoked trout

Peel oranges and segment over a bowl. Set segments aside and keep juice collected in bowl. Trim tops and root end of fennel. Reserve feathery tops. Slice fennel bulb in half lengthwise and remove core. Slice fennel lengthwise as thinly as possible and arrange fennel with orange segments on a platter. Combine olive oil with orange juice and pour over all. Sprinkle with black pepper, minced fennel tops, and toasted almonds, if desired. For an even more elegant salad, add some flaked smoked trout. (Decrease olive oil to 2 Tbsp. if using trout.)

Recipes © Amy Nathan Weber

Marketing manager Annabelle Lenderink helps customers at the Marin County Farmers' Market at the Civic Center

"It is very satisfying to be growing wonderful, tasty fruits and vegetables that are in harmony with nature, are good for the planet, and are held in such high regard by the consumer."

~ Warren Weber

The Historic "I" Ranch, also known as the McClure Ranch, is located on 1,400 acres of grasslands within Point Reyes National Seashore. Bob McClure, a fourth-generation dairy farmer, was raised right there. Today he runs the operation with his dad, Ron, and the help of a handful of employees who live on the ranch with their families.

The dairy operation has been in the McClure family since the late 1800s when Bob's great-grandfather James, straight from Ireland, began building his dream of having his own dairy. He was 18 years old. The business has changed locations over the last century, but has always remained in the hands of a McClure.

"I always knew I would keep this family tradition alive," says Bob. "I studied the dairy business at Cal Poly in San Luis Obispo and have been working here full-time since 1983."

Bob McClure in the field with his dairy cows

The dairy operation has been in the McClure family since the late 1800s when Bob's great-grandfather James, straight from Ireland, began building his dream of having his own dairy

Bob and his wife Ruth, who also hails from an agricultural family, and their three girls all enjoy being part of a dairy family. The oldest daughter, teenaged Jeannette, says she likes living in the country because "it's peaceful and there aren't many distractions." She is very involved in 4H and shows her rabbits, chickens, and occasionally a steer or two at both county and state fairs.

Rafael Gomez helps oversee the milking operation

The McClures milk 500 Holstein cows. "We've got two state-of-the-art barns which cover an area of more than an acre," says Bob. "We keep our cows inside the barns during the winter and turn them out to graze in the spring and summer months."

Bob is usually up by six in the morning and back at home by nine at night. He doesn't mind the hours because, unlike most urban dwellers, where he lives is where he works.

"I'm my own boss and I wouldn't change that for any other kind of job," says Bob. "If I want to take off in the middle of the day to take a field trip with my kids, I do it. I have great flexibility because I have a tremendous group of employees who are dedicated to this dairy operation."

"My kids were raised with the children of our employees. We all live next door to one another and if someone needs something, there are a lot of different doors they can open. There's a lot of security in that and it's a great way for children to grow up. It's how I was raised and it's how we are raising our girls. This ranch has given us an extraordinary sense of family."

Ron and Bob McClure

Jeannette McClure's Mocha Truffle Cheesecake

Crust:

1 pkg. devil's food cake mix

6 Tbsp. butter, melted

1 egg

1–3 Tbsp. instant coffee granules

In a mixing bowl, combine cake mix, butter, egg, and coffee granules. Press onto bottom and 2 inches up the sides of greased 10-inch spring form pan.

Filling:

2 pkgs. (8 oz. each) cream cheese, softened

1 can (14 oz.) sweetened condensed milk

2 cups (12 oz.) semisweet chocolate chips, melted

3–6 Tbsp. instant coffee granules

1/4 cup hot water

3 eggs, lightly beaten

In a mixing bowl, beat cream cheese until smooth. Beat in milk and chips. Dissolve coffee granules in hot water. Cool. Add coffee and eggs to cream cheese mixture; beat on low speed just until combined. Pour into crust. Place pan on a baking sheet. Bake at 325°F for 50–55 minutes until center is almost set. Cool on a wire rack for 10 minutes. Carefully run a knife around edge of pan to loosen; cool one hour longer. Chill overnight. Remove sides of pan before serving.

Above: Linda and Joey Mendoza with Audrey. *Below:* Joey at the computer, monitoring his cows

and I take care of the ones in maternity pens. We are milking twice a day, seven days a week. Our jobs don't end until nightfall."

"My grandparents started from scratch on this farm," hc says. "They spoke no English and made many sacrifices to get this operation going. We are continuing the tradition because we take pride in what we do and what we've always done. We believe that agriculture and families make for a very strong family unit. I can't imagine any other kind of life."

The tip of the Point Reyes Peninsula may seem a long way from the world of technology, but on the 1,200-acre Mendoza Family Ranch, milking cows can be as high-tech as it is hands-on.

Located on the Historic B Ranch within Point Reyes National Seashore, the dairy's 600 Holstein cows produce 4,000 gallons of milk each day. And everyday, a computer-run system lets dairyman Joey Mendoza and his crew monitor everything from how much each cow needs to be fed and how much milk she's producing, to when she should be sold. The computer even keeps track of when the feeding needs to change and when a calf will be born.

"Our lives are centered on the dairy," says Joey who has been at his job for more than 45 years. "I'm up at dawn to move the cows and to check to see how each one is doing. I know who's pregnant, who's in heat,

"We believe that agriculture and families make for a very strong family unit. I can't imagine any other kind of life."

~ Joey Mendoza

An opportunistic crow at the feeding trough on the Historic B Ranch

His 87-year-old father, Joe, still helps Joey run the dairy. His mother, Scotty, has been involved in the dairy business for all 64 years of her marriage. She's also famous in local circles for the handmade teddy bear baby quilts she sews for friends and family. Joey's sister Sharon Mendoza and her husband Steve own a dairy, a winery, and a bed-and-breakfast on their ranch located a few miles north of Pt. Reyes Station. A cousin operates a nearby dairy.

Joey, his wife Linda, and their two grown children all appreciate their agricultural heritage. "My kids have been herding cattle since they were three years old, and they plan to take over the operation when the time comes. Our families work together and practically live together because our dairies are all in West Marin." says Joey. "We have a wonderful quality of life because of what we do, and I feel thankful every day for that." 🍃

Linda's Lemon Square Pudding

Crust:

1/2 cup soft butter

1/2 cup salted cashews, finely ground

1 cup flour

Mix together and press into 13 x 9 x 2 inch pan. Bake at 375° F until light brown, about 15 minutes.

Filling:

1 cup powdered sugar

1 (8 oz.) pkg. cream cheese, softened

1/2 cup chilled whipped cream

2 (3 3/4 oz.) pkgs. lemon instant pudding

3 cups milk

1 Tbsp. grated lemon peel

Beat sugar and cream cheese until fluffy. Stir into whipped cream. Spread on cooled crust and refrigerate. Mix together pudding, milk, and grated lemon peel. Pour over cream cheese mixture. Refrigerate and serve cold topped with more whipped cream.

evin Lunny and his five siblings grew up on the Historic G Ranch on the Point Reyes Peninsula within Point Reyes National Seashore. Kevin's dad, Joe, ran his 1,500-acre ranch as a dairy farm until the 1970s. When costs seemed to outweigh profits, the family changed the operation from producing milk to producing beef.

"I loved growing up on this ranch," says Kevin, father of three teenaged children—triplets! "Our childhood was always very active and lively. We were always working on the ranch. By the time I was six, I was washing the barn, cleaning the corrals, and feeding the calves."

He says that being part of a working ranch was a tremendous family adventure. "The success of our business was totally dependent on the involvement of all of us. So, as kids, we always felt needed and important. We lived together, we worked together, and growing up, we ate three meals a day together. I wouldn't have changed that for any other kind of life."

Kevin, his wife Nancy, their children, and 200 head of Black Angus/Hereford mix all live on the ranch. His parents, Joe and Joan, practically live next door. Joe continues to work full-time as a cattleman (Kevin calls his dad his hero and credits him for "my love of this ranch and everything that goes with it"), but all the family members contribute to the success of the certified organic and certified grass-fed beef

Joan and Joe Lunny with son Kevin and daughter Ginny Cummings

"The success of our business was totally dependent on the involvement of all of us. So, as kids, we always felt needed and important."

~ Kevin Lunny

operation. Kevin's two brothers and three sisters and their families all help out during round-ups.

"My dad and grandfather ran the ranch until I was old enough to handle more responsibility," says Kevin who earned his degree in Animal Science from UC Davis. "And even though we've been through some hard times making ends meet, when money got tight, we got creative. We began to diversify."

One of those "creative" diversification solutions was organic artichokes. Another was oysters. And yet another was non-agricultural but practical—the launching of a paving company that Kevin runs with his two brothers.

We put in three acres of certified organic heirloom green globe artichokes in the summer of 2004," says Kevin. "Most people don't know it, but less than half a century ago, the Point Reyes Peninsula was the artichoke capitol of the state. Now we are reintroducing them to the area and are having some real success."

Also in 2004, the family purchased the former Johnson's Oyster Company on Drakes Estero. This aquaculture operation has become an almost full-time endeavor for Kevin and one that he is very excited about.

"My goal is to 'farm in the wild'," says Kevin. "We want to be environmentally sensitive, impact the land as little as possible, and focus on biodiversity. We need to keep our agricultural operations as local as possible and be less dependent on fossil fuel. I think we can grow and sell locally and be both sustainable and profitable. I see this is as the future of farming in Marin."

Kevin shucks oysters in his booth at the Saturday morning Pt. Reyes Farmers Market

Below: Nellie Gamez manages the oyster farm at Drakes Estero

Cream of Artichoke Soup
Serves 4

3 lbs. artichokes (3–4 medium, trimmed of thorns)	**2 cups chicken stock**
	1 tsp. ground pepper
	1 tsp. salt
4 cups water	**1/2 cup half-and-half**
1 Tbsp. olive oil	**1/2 cup 1% milk**
1 Tbsp. lemon juice	**Sprig of fresh thyme or**
4 garlic cloves, crushed	**1 tsp. dried thyme**

In a big soup pot, put the artichokes in water with oil, lemon juice, and two of the garlic cloves and cook 45 minutes. Drain, set aside the leaves, and discard choke. Put remaining artichoke hearts in food processor. Purée hearts with the stock, remaining garlic, salt, and pepper. Slice 1/2–1 cup of the tender end of the artichoke leaves into thin strips. Reheat the puree along with the artichoke leaves, half-and-half, milk, and thyme. Serve warm.

Left to right: Jill Giacomini Basch, Dean Giacomini, Bob Giacomini, Karen Giacomini Howard, and Lynn Giacomini Stray

Bob Giacomini's family has been involved in West Marin agriculture for three generations. Bob has operated a dairy business for more than 40 years on a 700-acre ranch overlooking Tomales Bay in Point Reyes Station. Today, his four daughters run the business with him—a dairy business that has evolved into one that makes cheese.

In 2000, Bob, his wife Dean, and their daughters decided they wanted to create an artisan blue cheese that would be handmade exclusively from milk from their own cows. It was something they were excited about because they knew they could do it as a family and make their mark as the only Californians making blue cheese. They called their new company Point Reyes Farmstead Cheese Company.

We were really eager to get this operation going," says Lynn Giacomini Stray, the company's managing partner. "But we couldn't do it on our own because making this kind of cheese requires someone who has vast experience with the mold, the process, and precision of producing a really first-class blue-veined cheese."

"My sisters and I love working together in this family operation. It gives us great balance, and it's a legacy we can pass on to the next generation." ~ Lynn Giacomini Stray

A national search brought the family to Monte McIntyre, who had been making blue cheese for the Maytag Cheese Company in Iowa. Ready to leave the corn-and soybean-covered landscape, McIntyre headed west with a promise to help the family make cheese from what grows and occurs naturally on the Giacomini ranch.

Today the fat wheels of Original Blue are processed, packaged, and shipped from a plant located fewer than 100 feet from where the cows graze and are milked. The cheese is sold locally as well as nationally, and the operation has become a family success story.

"My sisters and I love working together in this family operation," says Lynn. "We were all in marketing and sales, and this venture is a wonderful way to use our talents with something that we love. It gives us great balance, and it's a legacy we can pass on to the next generation." 🍃

Luis Mora *(foreground)* prepares the cheese for packaging

The Nutty Tuscan Pizza

Pizza dough for one 12–14 inch crust
8 oz. fresh mozzarella, thinly sliced
   or shredded
1 large yellow onion, caramelized
4–6 Roma tomatoes, roasted
2 cloves garlic, chopped

3/4–1 cup Farmstead Original Blue cheese
   crumbles (5 oz.)
2 tsp. toasted pine nuts
1/4 cup fresh basil, chopped
1/2 tsp. dried crushed red chili pepper, optional

Preheat oven and pizza stone or heavy cookie sheet to 475°F. Shape dough into a 12–14 inch round. Spread mozzarella evenly over dough, along with onions, tomatoes and garlic. Using a spatula, put the round on the pizza stone or cookie sheet, and bake until light brown, 8–10 minutes. Open oven and sprinkle blue cheese crumbles over pizza and bake 1–2 minutes more. Remove from oven, sprinkle with pine nuts and crushed red pepper and garnish with fresh basil.

Apple and Onion Chutney with Original Blue

2 Tbsp. butter
1 cup thinly sliced sweet onions
1 large Granny Smith apple, peeled,
   cored, and cut into matchsticks

1/3 cup brown sugar
1/3 cup rice vinegar
Salt and pepper to taste
6 oz. wedge Farmstead Original Blue cheese

Melt butter in heavy skillet. Add onions and apples; sauté 10 minutes or so until tender. Add brown sugar. Reduce heat and sauté until golden brown. Add vinegar and simmer until liquid is completely absorbed. Season with salt and pepper and cool completely. Serve with cheese and baguette toasts.

When Toby Giacomini opened Toby's Feed Barn in 1942, it was located in the Point Reyes Station barn that now houses the Cowgirl Creamery. In 1976, when Toby's son Chris took over the operation, he moved the enterprise to an old lumber warehouse on Highway One, the main street of town.

Today the hay barn market is probably one of the most unique and unusual retail operations in the county. Not only does Chris sell tons of hay and animal feed, but he also offers the public a rich variety of shopping and browsing opportunities and community events.

In fact, Toby's has everything from locally grown organic produce, cheeses, bottled milk, and olive oil to locally produced pet supplies, gardening tools, penny candies, crafts, greeting cards, and clothing. A sprawling art gallery features shows that change each month and include paintings, sculptures, photographs, student artwork, and contemporary installations.

Toby Giacomini, Sr. sits the front porch of Toby's Feed Barn

Inside the barn, Chris's son Nick and Nick's wife Amanda run a yoga studio where they teach classes every day. The stark contrast between the old barn filled with hay, firewood, and, often, cozy cages of baby chickens, and the sleek, modern yoga center offering yoga gear and natural lotions and oils is part of the charm of Toby's Feed Barn.

I get to work with my kids, see my dad rocking on the front porch, and sell things that are really good for the planet. How much better can it get?" ~ Chris Giacomini

"We're like an old-fashioned general store," says Chris. "We've got a little of everything. I like supporting our neighbors, so if they've baked or created something good and, hopefully, organic, I buy it."

"We're all about community and giving back. We've got a community garden, and our barn is used for everything from weddings and memorial services to Halloween parties and fundraisers."

Every Saturday from July through October, Toby's is the scene of a popular farmers' market. It began in 1998 when Sue Conley of Cowgirl Creamery spearheaded the effort to create a West Marin market featuring the products of local growers and producers. It has become a huge draw for both locals and visitors and is one of the only totally organic farmers' markets on the West Coast.

Chris waits on a customer in Toby's Feed Barn

naturally, Toby's. Chris's dad Toby, Sr. now passes his time out on the front porch, chatting with shoppers and flirting with the girls. This is definitely a family operation.

"I love the spirit of community in this town and the relationships I have with all my customers. I get behind the counter and really like waiting on people," says Chris. "Most of my employees have been here

Chris's other children, Adam and Melissa, are often at the market and work right alongside their dad. The hay Chris sells is baled and delivered in massive hay trucks operated by his brothers, Joe and Toby, Jr. The brothers run a sizeable fleet of hay trucks named,

for 14 or 15 years, and they are as much of Toby's as I am. I get to work with my kids, see my dad rocking on the front porch, and sell things that are really good for the planet. How much better can it get?"

Carole's Blackberry Cheese Pie

Chris's mom Vetalena, now in her mid-80's, offered this treasured family recipe.

8 oz. cream cheese
1 1/2 cups sugar
1 tsp. vanilla
1 cup whipping cream,
   preferably Straus Creamery

1 pie crust, store-bought
3 cups fresh organic blackberries
4 Tbsp. water
1 cup white sugar
3 Tbsp. corn starch

In a large bowl, whip cream cheese, sugar, and vanilla until thoroughly mixed and creamy. In a separate bowl, whip the cream until stiff and fold in with cream cheese mixture until smooth.

Bake the pie crust, cool, and put in the refrigerator until cold. In a saucepan, bring the blackberries to a boil, including all the juices plus 4 Tbsp. water and 1 cup sugar. Add the cornstarch, turn down heat, and simmer for 5–10 minutes. Cool.

Remove pie crust from refrigerator, add whipped cream mixture to the bottom, and pour blackberry mixture on top of that. Refrigerate overnight.

Cowgirl Creamery in Point Reyes Station is a producer of unique, prize-winning artisan cheeses, handmade from organic milk from the Straus Dairy in Marshall. The cheese is processed in open view at the company-owned Tomales Bay Foods Barn in downtown Pt. Reyes Station.

The cheesemaking venture was still a dream when Sue Conley, the co-owner and founder of the renowned Bette's Oceanview Diner in Berkeley (customers would wait in line for hours for their famous pancakes), wanted to make a change in her life. She wasn't alone. Her longtime friend Peggy Smith, an esteemed chef for 17 years at Chez Panisse, was looking for new possibilities as well. They moved to West Marin to figure out just what kind of business they wanted to create. There were many options, but two things were clear: it needed to be food-related and, ideally, locally produced.

The women bought an abandoned hay barn one block off the main street , remodeled it, and launched Tomales Bay Foods in 1993, selling a variety of local cheeses and food products. But the more they discovered the subtle tastes, flavors, and textures of artisan cheeses, they more interested they became in making their own.

They studied, researched, and traveled the world to learn the art of creating fine cheeses. When they realized that the one ingredient they needed most to make a world class cheese was right down the road at the Straus Dairy, they knew this was it. They would make locally-produced cheese using fresh, organic, locally produced milk. In February, 1997, Cowgirl Creamery was born.

Sue Conley and Peggy Smith

"The quality of the water, the air that surrounds the farm...and how the cows are fed and raised are critical to making the kind of cheese we produce."

~ Peggy Smith

Today the Cowgirls and their cheesemakers use 2,000 lbs. of organic, local milk each week to produce their artisan cheeses which are sold at their Pt. Reyes location and in their shop in San Francisco's newly renovated Ferry Building, "We always offer at least six different cheeses—three fresh cheeses and three aged, soft cheeses," says Peggy.

"We only use Straus organic milk because it has a very distinctive flavor that is perfect for our cheese profile," says Sue. "The quality of the water, the air that surrounds the farm (a few miles north of the creamery), and how the cows are fed and raised are critical to making the kind of cheese we produce."

Their hard work is paying off. Cowgirl Creamery won Best of Show for its Red Hawk cheese at the 2003 American Cheese Competition in San Francisco. In 2004, the company took home five ribbons for excellence in that same prestigious event (competing against 640 other renowned cheese makers) and won first prize for its Mt. Tam in the soft-ripened category.

Jonathan White expertly makes cheese at the Cowgirl Creamery

Sue says the best part of her job is the magic of it all. "I love the thrill of cheesemaking and creating the unique variations in flavor that emerge from each cheese. I also enjoy encouraging other small, good cheesemakers to get started and become successful. We're all in this together."

Peggy is adamant about promoting sustainable agriculture. "We are proving that you can use sustainable farming and business practices and make a good living at it."

When asked about their mentors, they both agreed that the late dairywoman Ellen Straus was instrumental in pioneering the organic movement in California and was one of the first and greatest supporters of their new venture. 🌱

Mt. Tam with Stone Fruit Compote
Serves 6

2 cups fruity white wine, such as Viognier
  or Gewurztraminer
1/4 cup sugar
1 cup pitted cherries
1/2 cup dried apricots, halved

3 peaches or nectarines, peeled and
  cut into 1/2 inch chunks
1 pkg. of Cowgirl Creamery Mt. Tam
  Triple-Cream Cheese
3 mint leaves, finely cut for garnish

Combine wine and sugar in medium saucepan over low heat. Stir until the sugar dissolves. Bring the mixture to a simmer and add fruit. Cook 5–8 minutes. Pour mixture through a strainer and reserve liquid; set fruit aside. Return liquid to saucepan and put over high heat. Reduce to 1/2 cup, about 20–25 minutes. Cool liquid to room temperature and pour over the reserved fruit. Put into a container and store in the refrigerator for at least one hour. Bring the Mt. Tam to room temperature and, when ready to serve, cut Mt. Tam into 12 slices—2 for each plate. Place cheese on dessert plates and ladle room temperature fruit over cheese. Garnish with mint chiffonade.

Conley & Smith photo:
Cowgirl Creamery

Jerry Draper balances a full-time job as a computer consultant with being an organic farmer. His farm is certainly not typical. It's right in the heart of San Anselmo, located just minutes away from the bustling traffic on Sir Francis Drake Boulevard.

Draper Farms is small, just one-half acre cut out of a 15-acre plot, but it's a lively operation, offering more than 50 different varieties of certified organic vegetables and a rich selection of nursery plants.

Jerry Draper with his dad, Jerry, Sr., works the San Anselmo organic farm

"It's the peace of mind that comes with what we are doing, the connection to what we are growing on this land, the people who harvest it, and the community that has grown up around it." ~ Jerry Draper

Jerry and his wife Mea bought the property in 1994 in order to build a house on the side of the hill. Jerry hadn't planned to become a farmer, but his father looked at the rich soil and suggested that he begin a small garden.

A lifelong conservationist, Jerry had studied organic gardening in urban settings at the University of California in the early 1970s, and he was fascinated by the possibilities. Little did he know that two decades later he would put what he had learned into practice.

Currently the Drapers only sell their produce through a Community Supported Agriculture (CSA) program. A small group of cooperative members pick and pay for what they need after learning the correct way to harvest. Recipes show them ways to prepare what they've just gathered.

Everything that the Drapers grow starts from heirloom seeds, some from strains centuries old. The soil is a rich mixture of compost, organic green sand, dairy manure, and other organic nutrients that help build the soil.

Jerry's father is a major player in the enterprise. Retired, he comes to the farm every day from March to October to plant, tend, and harvest. "This place is about family and community," says Jerry, Sr., who collects and writes all the recipes for the farm. "My wife, our kids, our grandkids, even the local pre-schoolers, all make this an extended family operation."

"I love working in this dirt," says Jerry, "but it's so much more than just the food we grow. It's the peace of mind that comes with what we are doing, the connection to what we are growing on this land, the people who harvest it, and the community that has grown up around it."

Tomatillo Salsa Verde

20 tomatillos	2 Tbsp. cilantro
2 jalapeno chilies	1/4 tsp sugar
1 yellow onion	salt to taste
1 clove garlic	2 Tbsp. olive oil

Husk and wash the tomatillos. Boil the tomatillos in a little water until tender. Drain, purée in blender, and set aside. Chop the remaining vegetables, and mince the cilantro. Heat the oil in a skillet. Add the vegetables, the puréed tomatillos, sugar, and salt. Cook and stir over medium heat for 5 minutes. Cool and serve. Refrigerate or freeze.

Cucumber Vichyssoise

3 Tbsp. green onions	1/2 cup celery
3 Tbsp. yellow onions	3/4 cup parsley
1 Tbsp. shallots	2 Tbsp. butter

Chop all ingredients and sauté in butter until soft.

3 cups chicken stock	1/4 cup watercress, chopped
3 cups potatoes, diced	1/4 tsp thyme

Add to first mixture. Bring to a boil, then reduce heat and simmer, covered, until potatoes are soft, about 20 minutes. Cool slightly.

1 large cucumber, peeled, seeded, and grated	Dash of Tabasco
	Splash of half-and-half cream
2 cups sour cream	Chopped parsley for garnish
1/4 tsp salt	

Add everything except the half-and-half cream to above mixture. Purée in blender, thinning with half-and-half, as necessary. Chill. Garnish with chopped parsley and serve.

Marin County Agricultural Lands

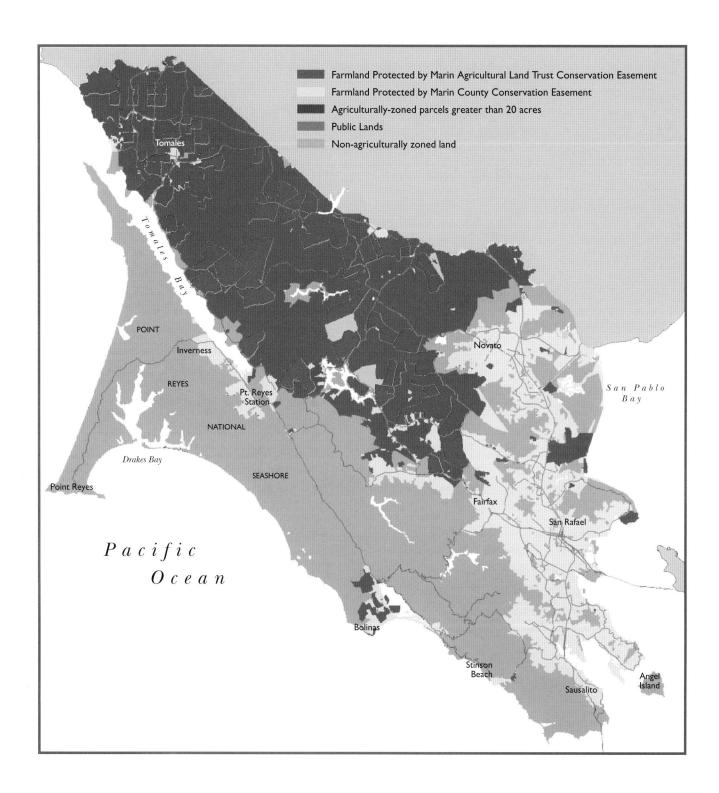

Farmland Protected by Marin Agricultural Land Trust Conservation Easement
Farmland Protected by Marin County Conservation Easement
Agriculturally-zoned parcels greater than 20 acres
Public Lands
Non-agriculturally zoned land

Tomales

Tomales Bay

POINT

Inverness

Novato

REYES

San Pablo Bay

Pt. Reyes
Station

NATIONAL

Drakes Bay

SEASHORE

Point Reyes

Fairfax

San Rafael

*Pacific
Ocean*

Bolinas

Stinson
Beach

Angel
Island

Sausalito

Resources for Farm Products

The following family farms and ranches grow, produce, and sell their food products locally:

Chileno Valley Ranch *chilenobeef.com*
Products sold exclusively on premises by reservation only.

Corda Ranch *cordawinery.com*
Wines sold at markets throughout Marin including Scotty's in San Rafael, Bruno's in San Rafael, or at the winery by reservation only.

Straus Dairy *strausmilk.com*
Dairy products sold at markets throughout Marin including Toby's Feed Barn in Point Reyes Station, Whole Foods, and Mollie Stone's.

Hog Island Oyster Company *hogislandoyster.com*
Oysters sold at markets throughout Marin including Whole Foods, Hog Island Oyster Company in Marshall, and Hog Island Oyster Bar & Restaurant at the San Francisco Ferry Plaza.

Little Organic Farm
Products sold at Marin Civic Center Farmers' Market and San Francisco Ferry Plaza Farmers' Market.

Marin Sun Farms *marinsunfarms.com*
Products sold at Marin Civic Center Farmers' Market, San Francisco Ferry Plaza Farmers' Market, and Marin Sun Farms Butcher Shop and Eatery in Point Reyes Station.

Allstar Organics *allstarorganics.com*
Products sold at markets throughout Marin including Woodlands Market in Kentfield, Allstar Farm Stand in Nicasio (seasonal), and San Francisco Ferry Plaza Farmers' Market.

Cow Track Ranch *cowtrack.net*
Produce sold at Toby's Feed Barn in Point Reyes Station and Marin Art and Garden Farm Stand in Ross.

McEvoy Ranch *mcevoyranch.com*
Olive oils sold at markets throughout Marin including Whole Foods, United Markets, and McEvoy Ranch Shop at San Francisco Ferry Plaza.

Star Route Farms *starroutefarms.com*
Produce sold at markets throughout Marin including Marin Civic Center Farmers' Market, Star Route Farm Stand in Bolinas (seasonal), and San Francisco Ferry Plaza Farmers' Market.

Robert Giacomini Dairy *Point Reyes Farmstead Cheese Company* *pointreyescheese.com*
Products sold at markets throughout Marin including Scotty's in San Rafael, Whole Foods, and United Markets.

Cowgirl Creamery *cowgirlcreamery.com*
Products sold at markets throughout Marin including Woodlands Market, Cowgirl Creamery in Point Reyes Station, and Cowgirl Creamery shop at San Francisco Ferry Plaza.

Draper Farms *onthefarm.net*
Produce can be purchased on the farm by reservation only.

Marin Agricultural Land Trust

Marin Agricultural Land Trust is a leader in the conservation movement in the United States. As the first agricultural land trust in the nation, MALT has created a legacy of innovation that inspires farmland protection efforts from Vermont to Hawaii.

In Marin County, agriculture has been a way of life for more than 150 years. MALT was founded during a time when that way of life and the land that nurtured it were both threatened. Not so long ago, it looked as if West Marin would become a suburb of San Francisco. Plans for highways through pastureland, for a big city on the shores of Tomales Bay, and for typical urban development came close to being approved. West Marin would have been changed forever.

Thanks to the vision of dairywoman Ellen Straus, wetlands biologist Phyllis Faber, and a group of dedicated ranchers and environmentalists, that didn't happen. Today, Marin farms produce milk, cheese, butter, beef, oysters, olive oil, and wine grapes, plus fruit and vegetable crops that are widely praised for their quality. These farmlands also provide important wildlife habitat and incomparable scenic vistas.

"We don't take the vision of our founders for granted," says Executive Director Robert Berner. "MALT has protected 57 family farms and ranches and 38,000 acres in the past 25 years—more than one-third of the farmland in the County! But 80,000 acres are still at risk."

Even after a quarter century of work by MALT, threats to Marin farmland and agriculture persist. MALT is a membership organization that depends on its supporters to help protect these lands and the production of healthy food, close to home.

....

Marin Agricultural Land Trust
Robert Berner, Executive Director
Post Office Box 809
Point Reyes Station, CA 94956
415.663.1158
www.malt.org

Marin Agricultural Land Trust
has protected 38,000 acres
of irreplaceable farmland on
57 family farms and ranches
Photo: Elisabeth Ptak
Agricultural Partner Organizations
stories written by Elisabeth Ptak

The 400-member Marin County Farm Bureau is part of a 90,000-strong statewide organization that develops solutions to problems that affect the lives of farming families. From production to land use, from labor issues to marketing and environmental concerns, its mission is to represent all aspects of agriculture in Marin County while providing protection and enhancement of local agriculture.

"Agriculture is an industry that includes a way of life," says Sally Pozzi, current Marin County Farm Bureau president. Her husband has served in that role in the past. "Besides providing food in an environmentally responsible way, its multi-generational families help make Marin County the wonderful place it is to live. Family farms and ranches provide beautiful views and have protected the vast rolling hills close to San Francisco from development. Marin County agriculture provides a safe, affordable, locally grown food supply. It generates jobs, habitat for wildlife, tax revenues, and stable communities."

Farm Bureau members also help staff the annual chicken barbecue on Western Weekend in Pt. Reyes Station. They also collaborate with organizations like Marin Agricultural Land Trust and Marin Organic on outreach activities to educate the public about the benefits and challenges of family farming in the county.

Each year, the Marin County Farm Bureau joins with other local organizations to sponsor the Junior Livestock Show on Western Weekend in Pt. Reyes Station where boys and girls from the surrounding areas compete with their animals for awards in several categories

Marin County Farm Bureau
Sally Pozzi, President
Post Office Box 219
Point Reyes CA 94956
415-663-1231
www.cfbf.com

Photo: Elisabeth Ptak

The Marin County Farmers' Market Association was founded in 1983 with a goal of creating a place to educate, connect, and support farmers and communities. It does that now, year round, at twice-weekly markets at the Civic Center and seasonally in Novato and Fairfax. "Our present and future goal is to showcase all of Marin's farmers, ranchers, and dairymen whether they are organic, transitioning to organic, or using conventional production methods," explains Executive Director Brigitte Moran. "We want to be a platform for Marin's agriculture, an exhibit, a classroom and, most of all, we hope to reflect the spirit of farming."

While the current markets provide easy access to farm products once or twice a week, a site that would be open daily could benefit both farmers and consumers. "We believe Marin is ripe for a permanent home for our farmers," says Brigitte, describing the Marin Center for Sustainable Agriculture proposed at the Civic Center. "It will be a place where you can buy Marin beef in our butcher shop, fish in our fish shop, milk, and cheese, and fresh baked goods," she says.

In the meantime, the markets will continue to be a source of regional sustainable farm products for consumers and a viable market for farmers. Buying locally grown food directly from farmers provides both nutritional and economic benefits, and it unites farmers and communities as we get to know the hand—and the land—that feeds us. 🌿

....

Marin County Farmers' Market Association
Brigitte Moran, Executive Director
76 San Pablo Ave.
San Rafael, CA 94903
415-472-6100
www.marincountyfarmersmarkets.org

YEAR-ROUND MARKETS
Marin County Civic Center
Sunday 8AM–1PM
Thursday 8AM–1PM

SEASONAL MARKETS
Novato Tuesday 5–8PM
   April–September
Fairfax Wednesday 4–8PM
   May–October

Marin Food Systems Project

The Marin Food Systems Project is a broad coalition of teachers, parents, students, and community leaders who have come together to transform the relationship between schools and healthy food, between students and their health, and between schools and the local food system.

Marin students harvest vegetables from their school gardens

"We feel there is a critical connection between a healthy diet and a student's ability to learn effectively and achieve high standards in school," says Project Director Leah Smith. "Our role is to support Marin County agriculture by bringing about systemic changes in how local schools relate to local farms."

The Project provides the following services:

- Educational and networking meetings
- Professional development for teachers
- Food Service Director education
- School garden consultation
- Connections with local farms for food and educational opportunities
- School food policy technical assistance

The Project is a collaborative effort between dozens of partners working countywide with 35 Marin schools. Partners include: Marin Agricultural Land Trust; Marin Agriculture and Education Alliance; Marin Organic; UC Cooperative Extension Marin County; Marin County Health and Human Services/Nutrition Wellness Program; Marin Conservation Corps; Marin County Office of Education; and Good Earth Natural and Organic Foods.

"Food is our most fundamental connection to the land and provides a daily reminder of our interdependence with the natural world," says Leah Smith. "Local agriculture and a sustainable food supply are key to healthy and sustainable communities. Local farms support our economy, provide nutritious and fresh foods, create open space and habitat, and protect our environment."

Marin Food Systems Project
(A project of the Environmental Education Council of Marin)
Leah Smith, Project Director
1005 A Street, Suite 202
San Rafael, CA 94901
415.485.4908
http://www.eecom.net/projects_school.htm

Photos: Marin Food Systems Project

M arin Organic is at the forefront of a movement which is creating a healthy, sustainable, and safe environment for all beings today and for generations to come," says Executive Director Helge Hellberg.

Founded in 1999, Marin Organic focuses on the environmental soundness and economic viability of farming and ranching in Marin County. The organization promotes local organic agriculture by offering hands-on marketing support to its growers, plus events, exhibits, and farm tours for the public. In addition, Marin Organic has a variety of projects that address community health, such as the Organic School Lunch Program and a Community-Supported Agriculture (CSA) box program in underserved communities in Marin County. It also sponsors programs about environmental issues, including Salmon Safe certification for farmers who adopt fish-friendly conservation practices and participate in salmon habitat restoration.

"The organization is committed to creating the first all-organic county in the nation, a county in which growers and the people who rely on them recognize their mutual interdependence," says Hellberg. "By restoring ecological and social values to agriculture and realigning traditional expectations of farming with a holistic understanding of ecology, Marin Organic aims to re-empower local communities, foster environmentally sound agriculture, and celebrate local food production."

Marin Organic members include such well-known names such as: Cowgirl Creamery, makers of award-winning organic cheese; Star Route Farms, the oldest continuously certified organic farm in California; Straus Family Creamery, the first organic dairy west of the Mississippi; and Lunny Ranch, the first certified organic grass-fed beef operation in Marin. 🌿

Marin Organic
Helge Hellberg, Executive Director
Post Office Box 962
Point Reyes Station, CA 94956
415.663.9667
www.marinorganic.org

In November, 2005, the Prince of Wales and the Duchess of Cornwall visited the Point Reyes Farmers' Market. Marin Organic and its director, Helge Hellberg, coordinated the event which was a confirmation that Marin County agriculture is of critical importance far beyond the county line

Photo: Marin Organic

The Marin Resource Conservation District (MRCD) was founded in 1959 to assist agricultural landowners in their attempts to make the most efficient use of their farms and ranches. The District assists with erosion control and restoration projects and brings in funding from public agencies to help private landowners conserve soil and water resources.

"It is our belief that the health of the County's natural landscape is dependent upon a robust agricultural economy and the active preservation of our agricultural heritage," says Executive Director Nancy Scolari. "In addition, it is our firm conviction that the agricultural productivity of the County is dependent upon the diligent application of practices that conserve and enhance our natural resources."

The District serves landowners at their request, says Nancy. "We believe that this grassroots approach is in line with the best of American traditions, and that gradually but surely, excellent conservation accomplishments will be made through education, friendly persuasion, and cooperative action."

Besides helping local landowners, MRCD's program benefits the immediate community and the public at large. In the past 20 years, the group has administered more than $6 million dollars in government and private foundation grants for watershed-wide erosion

MRCD works with students to restore a gully with native plants to help prevent further erosion

control and restoration projects. Other MRCD functions include: agricultural land conservation; watershed planning and management; water conservation; soil and water quality protection and enhancement; wildlife habitat enhancement; wetland conservation; and conservation education.

Marin Resource Conservation District
Nancy Scolari, Executive Director
Post Office Box 1146
Point Reyes Station CA 94956
415.663.1170
www.sonomamarinrcds.org

Photo: MRCD

Point Reyes Seashore Ranchers Association

Agriculture has thrived in West Marin since the mid-19th century when the Californios, the first Mexican land grantees, settled here. The Point Reyes Penninsula became known as the birthplace of the California dairy industry and during the Gold Rush, it was famous for the "other" gold—butter—produced here and shipped by train or schooner to cities and towns throughout the West. Immigrants from Ireland, Switzerland, Portugal, Italy, and other countries established family farms that are still a vital part of the local economy.

Round-up time on the Grossi Ranch in Point Reyes National Seashore

Point Reyes National Seashore was established in 1972, and the ranches within its boundaries were purchased by the National Park Service, then leased back to their former owners. They continue today not only as an economic factor in our county and state, but as a living cultural resource.

The Point Reyes Seashore Ranchers Association is a volunteer organization of historic ranching families seeking to protect agricultural interests in Point Reyes National Seashore and Golden Gate National Recreation Area. The association's members strive to facilitate a healthy relationship between the National Park Service and agriculturalists who lease lands inside the park. "We also hope to educate the public on the stewardship of the land by local ranchers," says Anne Murphy who lives on the historic Home Ranch. Membership is open to anyone who operates an agricultural operation within Point Reyes National Seashore or Golden Gate National Recreation Area and their family members.

....

Point Reyes Seashore Ranchers' Association
Contact: Kevin Lunny
P.O. Box 1403
Point Reyes Station, CA 94956
415.669.1209

Photo: Elisabeth Ptak

The University of California Cooperative Extension (UCCE) has been operating in Marin County since 1921. "The office acts as a bridge to the UC system, bringing its research and knowledge to Marin residents," says Executive Director Ellie Rilla. "Our mission in Marin includes working to sustain agriculture, protecting our unique environmental heritage, and helping communities shape wise public policy by strengthening participation and leadership skills in youth and adults."

Also known as the County Farm Advisor's Office, UCCE works with producers, industry, county government, resource agencies, and community groups to preserve and support a healthy and sustainable agricultural industry in Marin and the region.

Watershed and range advisors help promote and diversify Marin agriculture. They protect the water quality in West Marin watersheds, and they deal with animal health & welfare issues. An Environmental Horticulture advisor provides integrated pest management information and education to the landscape industry, and coordinates research and education on Sudden Oak Death and other plant diseases. Volunteer Master Gardeners provide community service at schools, community gardens, farmers' markets, and other public spaces.

The 4-H Youth Development program offers nutrition and gardening education and curricular materials in selected schools. It provides hands-on, project-based learning in science literacy and leadership, therapeutic horseback riding, camping and outdoor adventure, and small pet care in community clubs throughout the county.

Steve Quirt, Organic and Sustainable Agriculture Coordinator for UC Cooperative Extension, works with farmers and ranchers to diversify their businesses

UCCE received the 2003 Marin Economic Commission Award of Excellence for Agricultural Viability. The citation was given for efforts to encourage agricultural product diversification and for helping to create market and brand recognition for Marin producers through the Grown in Marin program.

....

University of California Cooperative Extension
Ellie Rilla, Executive Director
1682 Novato Blvd.
Novato, CA 94947
415.499.4204
cemarin.ucdavis.edu
www.growninmarin.org

Photo: UC Cooperative Extension

Barbara Marino, *Writer*

Barbara is a writer, publicist and former art teacher. She spent her childhood in New Orleans, her teens in Arizona and became a grown-up in San Francisco. Barbara collects vintage cookbooks, Southwest Indian baskets and pottery, and loves living in San Rafael.

Susan Bercu, *Designer*

My mission—to create a framework for the warmly told stories of Barbara Marino—was also to honor Marin's farm families by bringing their messages to the wider community. Photographer Ken Smith, my intrepid fellow traveler in life, and I crisscrossed the magnificent hills and valleys of Marin County to visually record the farmers in their home environments. Their enduring equation of family, community, work, and nature guided the design of this book.

(*Left to right*) Barbara Marino and Susan Bercu

An award-winning graphic designer, illustrator and fine artist, Susan lives and works in San Rafael, serving Bay Area and national clients. www.bercudesign.com

Ken Smith, *Photographer*

When the designer of this book, who is also my wife, suggested the need for photos of the families featured in it, I couldn't wait to get started. Driving all the previously untravelled roads, lanes and cow tracks to meet, get to know, and photograph the guardians of Marin's agricultural heritage has been the best location assignment of my photographic career. It is the farmers, ranchers, and stewards of the land who truly hold the agricultural future of Marin in their dirt- stained hands. Thanks to them all for their hospitality, openness, and patience.

Ken Smith has a commercial photography studio in San Rafael with clients from the Bay Area and beyond. www.kensmithphotography.com

Elisabeth Ptak, *Editor*

The food we eat, the views that inspire us, even the wildlife habitat, all grow from the history and tradition of generations of people whose livelihood depended on careful stewardship of the lands of western Marin County. The stories of these ranching families are compelling because they help define the sense of place that is so important to all of us who love Marin County.

Elisabeth Ptak is the Associate Director and Director of Outreach for Marin Agricultural Land Trust. She also writes the weekly column "Homeward Bound" for the *Point Reyes Light*.